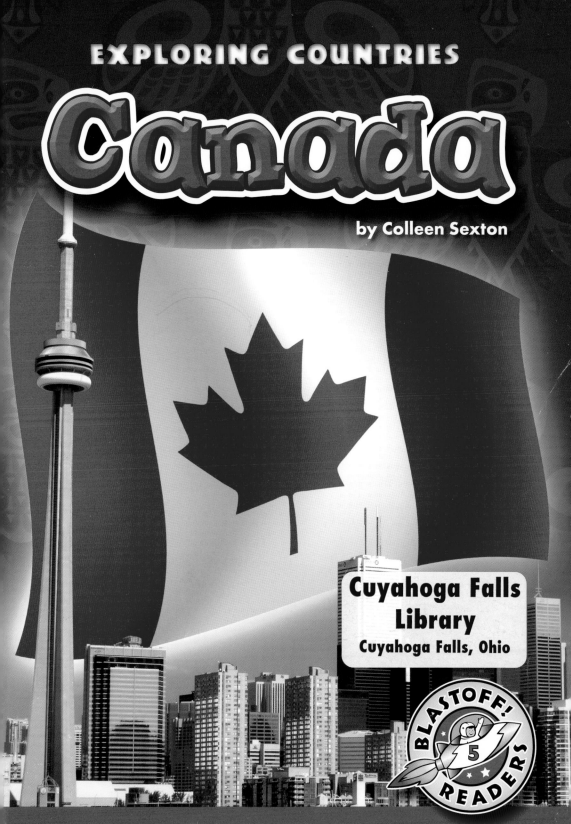

EXPLORING COUNTRIES

Canada

by Colleen Sexton

BLASTOFF! 5 READERS

BELLWETHER MEDIA · MINNEAPOLIS, MN

Note to Librarians, Teachers, and Parents:

Blastoff! Readers are carefully developed by literacy experts and combine standards-based content with developmentally appropriate text.

Level 1 provides the most support through repetition of high-frequency words, light text, predictable sentence patterns, and strong visual support.

Level 2 offers early readers a bit more challenge through varied simple sentences, increased text load, and less repetition of high-frequency words.

Level 3 advances early-fluent readers toward fluency through increased text and concept load, less reliance on visuals, longer sentences, and more literary language.

Level 4 builds reading stamina by providing more text per page, increased use of punctuation, greater variation in sentence patterns, and increasingly challenging vocabulary.

Level 5 encourages children to move from "learning to read" to "reading to learn" by providing even more text, varied writing styles, and less familiar topics.

Whichever book is right for your reader, Blastoff! Readers are the perfect books to build confidence and encourage a love of reading that will last a lifetime!

This edition first published in 2011 by Bellwether Media, Inc.

No part of this publication may be reproduced in whole or in part without written permission of the publisher. For information regarding permission, write to Bellwether Media, Inc., Attention: Permissions Department, 5357 Penn Avenue South, Minneapolis, MN 55419.

Library of Congress Cataloging-in-Publication Data

Sexton, Colleen A., 1967-
Canada / by Colleen Sexton.
    p. cm. – (Blastoff! readers: Exploring countries)
Includes bibliographical references and index.
Summary: "Developed by literacy experts for students in grades three through seven, this book introduces young readers to the geography and culture of Canada"–Provided by publisher.
ISBN 978-1-60014-475-2 (hardcover : alk. paper)
1. Canada–Juvenile literature. I. Title.
F1008.2.S38 2010
971–dc22
                                    2010006424

Text copyright © 2011 by Bellwether Media, Inc. BLASTOFF! READERS and associated logos are trademarks and/or registered trademarks of Bellwether Media, Inc.

Printed in the United States of America, North Mankato, MN.

080110   1162

Contents

Arctic
Ocean

Pacific
Ocean

Hudson
Bay

Canada

Ottawa

Great Lakes

United States

Canada is a country in North America that touches three oceans. With an area of 3,855,103 square miles (9,984,670 square kilometers), it stretches from the Atlantic Ocean in the east to the Pacific Ocean in the west. Canada also reaches north to the cold Arctic Ocean. It's no wonder that Canada's **motto** is "From Sea to Sea"!

Atlantic Ocean

! **fun fact**
Canada's coastline is 151,019 miles (243,042 kilometers) long. That's more coastline than any other country in the world!

Hudson Bay reaches into Canada from the Atlantic Ocean. Four of the five **Great Lakes** lie on Canada's southern border. The United States is Canada's neighbor to the south and northwest. Canada is divided into ten **provinces** and three **territories**. Its capital is Ottawa.

Canada's landscape varies greatly from coast to coast. In the east, rocky shoreline gives way to rolling hills. Farmland spreads across **lowlands** in the southeast. The **Canadian Shield** covers much of eastern and central Canada. There, a thin layer of soil lies on top of a thick layer of rock. The area has dense forests and many clear lakes.

In the west, fields of wheat stretch across open **prairies**. Tall mountain ranges rise west of the prairies. Mountainsides covered with forests slope down to the Pacific shore. Long, narrow inlets of water called **fjords** cut into the rocky Pacific coastline.

fjord

The Bay of Fundy on Canada's Atlantic coast has the highest tides in the world. At low tide, the water moves away from shore. At high tide, the water rises again. The difference in the water level between high tide and low tide can be as much as 56 feet (17 meters)!

! fun fact

Central Canada is dinosaur territory! Dinosaurs roamed this area more than 75 million years ago. Today, people can hunt for dinosaur bones in Dinosaur Provincial Park.

Canada's far north lies in the Arctic. Some islands in this area have tall mountains topped with glaciers. These sheets of ice and snow creep slowly toward the sea. Most of the Arctic is **tundra**. This flat, treeless land is frozen most of the year. The winters are very cold, and it is dark almost all the time. The tundra changes when summer and sunlight return to the Arctic. The top layer of earth thaws and colorful flowers bloom. In summer, the sun is even out in the middle of the night!

Did you know?

Baffin Island in the Arctic has more than 10,000 glaciers! Giant icebergs break off the glaciers when they meet the sea.

! fun fact

For hundreds of years, people in the Arctic have built *inuksuks* on the bare tundra. These stone landmarks show direction or mark hunting grounds.

moose

fun fact

Forests on the Pacific coast have trees that are more than 1,000 years old! The trees are over 300 feet (91 meters) tall and 13 feet (4 meters) wide.

Canada is famous for its wildlife. The country's forests give shelter to elk, moose, wolves, and foxes. Grizzly bears and cougars hunt on mountain slopes. Bighorn sheep roam the mountain peaks.

polar bear

killer whale

wolf

The cold Arctic is home to polar bears, musk oxen, and caribou. Beavers cut down trees near lakes and rivers. Killer whales, seals, and walruses swim in the nearby oceans. Puffins and blue herons nest on the Atlantic coast.

Canada is home to about 34 million people. They come from many backgrounds. Most people have **ancestors** who came from France, Great Britain, or Ireland. Other large groups came from Germany, Italy, and Ukraine.

Did you know?

Nunavut means "our land" in the Inuit language. Nunavut became a Canadian territory in 1999. About half of all Inuits in Canada live in Nunavut.

In recent years, many people have arrived from China, India, and the Philippines. Native peoples have lived in Canada for thousands of years. Today, **First Nations** people and **Inuits** make up only a small part of the population.

Did you know?

The largest cities are in warmer, southern parts of Canada. Almost three out of four Canadians live less than 100 miles (161 kilometers) from the U.S. border.

Many Canadians live in houses or apartments in Toronto, Montréal, Vancouver, or other large cities. They drive cars, take the bus, or ride the subway to get to work, supermarkets, and shopping malls. People also live in small towns or on family farms in the countryside. Communities in the Arctic are far apart. The Canadians who live there rely on the Internet for shopping, banking, and schooling.

Where People Live in Canada

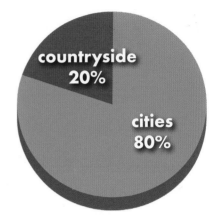

countryside 20%

cities 80%

! fun fact

There are few roads between towns in the Arctic. People use snowmobiles to get around in winter. In summer, they use boats and airplanes.

Canadians start school when they are 5 years old. In grade school, they study reading, math, science, and social studies. Students take art classes, learn how to use computers, and go on field trips. After eighth grade, students go to high school. They choose classes that will get them ready for universities or jobs. In the province of Québec, classes are taught in both French and English.

Did you know?

First Nations and Inuit children often learn to speak native languages in their neighborhood schools.

Working

Did you know?

Ships carry goods from ports on the Great Lakes to the St. Lawrence Seaway. This important waterway in southeastern Canada takes ships to the Atlantic Ocean.

Where People Work in Canada

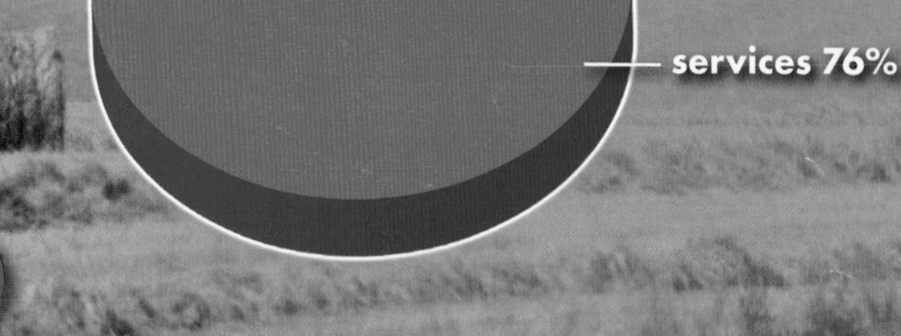

construction 6%

manufacturing 13%

farming 2%

other 3%

services 76%

More than half of Canadian workers hold **service jobs**. They work in banks, hospitals, stores, and government offices. Other Canadians work in factories making parts for cars and airplanes. Canada's **natural resources** provide many jobs. Loggers cut down trees that are made into paper and lumber. Farmers grow grains, fruits, and vegetables in the rich soil. Fishermen bring in catches of lobster, shrimp, and herring. Miners dig up nickel, diamonds, gold, and other **minerals**. People around the world use goods shipped from Canada's **ports**.

In their free time, Canadians visit friends, watch TV, and listen to music. They go to movies, museums, and zoos. In summer, Canadians camp and hike in more than 40 national parks. They go swimming, boating, and fishing.

The long, cold winters don't keep Canadians indoors. They go ice-skating, snowmobiling, skiing, and snowboarding. They also play hockey, which is the country's most popular sport. Many Canadians learn to ice-skate at an early age and play hockey all their lives.

fun fact

In winter, the frozen Rideau Canal in Ontario is the world's largest skating rink. It is nearly 5 miles (8 kilometers) long!

! **fun fact**

The maple syrup you pour on your pancakes might be from Canada! Canadians make most of the world's maple syrup.

Canadians eat a wide variety of foods. The oceans provide fresh seafood. Clam chowder and salmon dishes are popular. French Canadians eat a meat pie called *tourtière*. In the province of New Brunswick, people cook up fiddlehead ferns. Caribou and moose dishes are often served in the far north. Maple syrup on snow is a treat during the maple sap harvest in the spring. People throughout Canada eat *poutine*. This dish features french fries covered with gravy and cheese curds. Restaurants offer food from around the world. Canadians enjoy French, Greek, Italian, and Chinese dishes.

salmon

clam chowder

Canadians celebrate many holidays, including Halloween, Christmas, and New Year's Day. Canadians celebrate Thanksgiving in October. They gather for a special meal that usually includes turkey and pumpkin pie. Canadians come together on July 1 for Canada Day. They celebrate the day in 1867 that Canada became a country. People have picnics and parades. At night, fireworks light up the sky.

Montréal, Québec

fun fact

Road signs in many parts of Canada are written in both English and French.

English and French are Canada's two official languages. Most Canadians speak English. About one out of five Canadians speaks French. Most French-speaking Canadians live in Québec. They work to keep their language and way of life alive in Canada. Some people who live in Québec want it to become a separate country. Other Canadians want Québec to stay a part of Canada. They believe it is an important part of Canadian history, tradition, and culture.

Speak French!

English	French	How to say it
hello	bonjour	bohn-JOOR
good-bye	au revoir	oh ruh-VWAHR
yes	oui	WHEE
no	non	NOH
please	s'il vous plaît	SEEL VOO PLAY
thank you	merci	mayr-SEE
friend (male)	ami	ah-MEE
friend (female)	amie	ah-MEE

Québec

Fast Facts About Canada

Canada's Flag

Canada's flag is red and white. Red stands for England and white stands for France. People from these two countries were Canada's first European settlers. The maple leaf in the middle of the flag is a symbol of Canada. The country has used this flag since 1965.

Official Name: Canada

Area: 3,855,103 square miles (9,984,670 square kilometers); Canada is the 2nd largest country in the world.

Capital City:	Ottawa
Important Cities:	Toronto, Montréal, Vancouver, Edmonton
Population:	33,759,742 (July 2010)
Official Languages:	English and French
National Holiday:	Canada Day (July 1)
Religions:	Roman Catholic (42.6%), Protestant (23.3%), None (16%), Other (18.1%)
Major Industries:	energy, fishing, forestry, manufacturing, mining, services
Natural Resources:	iron ore, nickel, zinc, copper, gold, diamonds, silver, fish, timber, coal, oil, natural gas
Manufactured Products:	cars, airplane parts, wood and paper products, petroleum products, food products
Farm Products:	wheat, barley, fruits, vegetables, dairy products
Unit of Money:	Canadian dollar; the dollar is divided into 100 cents.

Glossary

ancestors—relatives who lived long ago

Canadian Shield—a rocky land area that covers more than half of Canada and is topped by a thin layer of soil; this area has pine forests and thousands of lakes.

First Nations—people whose ancestors lived in Canada before European explorers arrived; there are more than 600 First Nations groups in Canada.

fjords—long, narrow inlets of water between steep cliffs; fjords are formed by the movement of glaciers.

Great Lakes—large freshwater lakes on the border between Canada and the United States; the Great Lakes are Superior, Michigan, Huron, Erie, and Ontario; Lake Michigan is the only lake that doesn't touch Canada.

Hudson Bay—a large bay in northeastern Canada that connects to the Atlantic Ocean

Inuits—native people who live mostly in Canada's Arctic

lowlands—areas of land that are lower than the surrounding land

minerals—elements found in nature; gold, iron, and oil are examples of minerals.

motto—a saying that describes the beliefs or purpose of a person, group, or place

natural resources—materials in the earth that are taken out and used to make products or fuel

ports—sea harbors where ships can dock; ships leave Canada's ports to bring goods to the rest of the world.

prairies—large areas of flat, grassy land

provinces—areas within a country; provinces follow all the laws of the country and make some of their own laws.

service jobs—jobs that perform tasks for people or businesses

territories—areas of land that belong to a country

tundra—frozen, treeless land; beneath the surface, tundra is permafrost, or land that is permanently frozen.

To Learn More

AT THE LIBRARY

Aloian, Molly. *Canada Day*. New York, N.Y.:
Crabtree Publishing, 2010.

Bowers, Vivien. *That's Very Canadian!: An
Exceptionally Interesting Report About All Things
Canadian*. Toronto, Ont.: Maple Tree Press, 2004.

Kalman, Bobbie. *Spotlight on Canada*. New York,
N.Y.: Crabtree Publishing, 2008.

ON THE WEB

Learning more about Canada
is as easy as 1, 2, 3.

1. Go to www.factsurfer.com.

2. Enter "Canada" into the search box.

3. Click the "Surf" button and you will see a list of
   related Web sites.

With factsurfer.com, finding more information is just
a click away.

Index